YOU CAN BE RICH TOO!

By
X'ernona Woods

Chapter 1

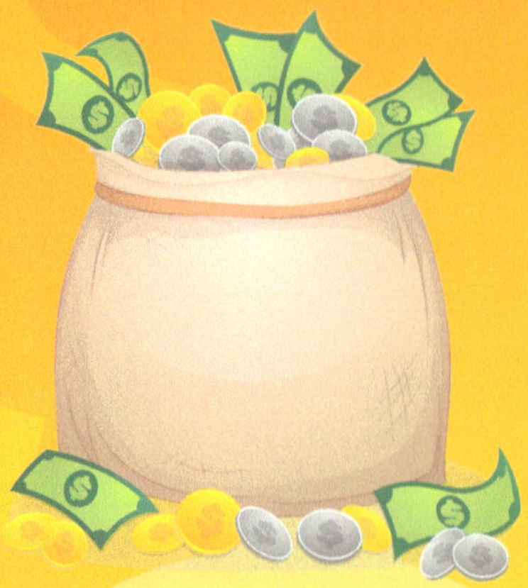

Money Language

Everyone speaks a different language. There are lots of languages that people speak, but have you ever heard of the money language?

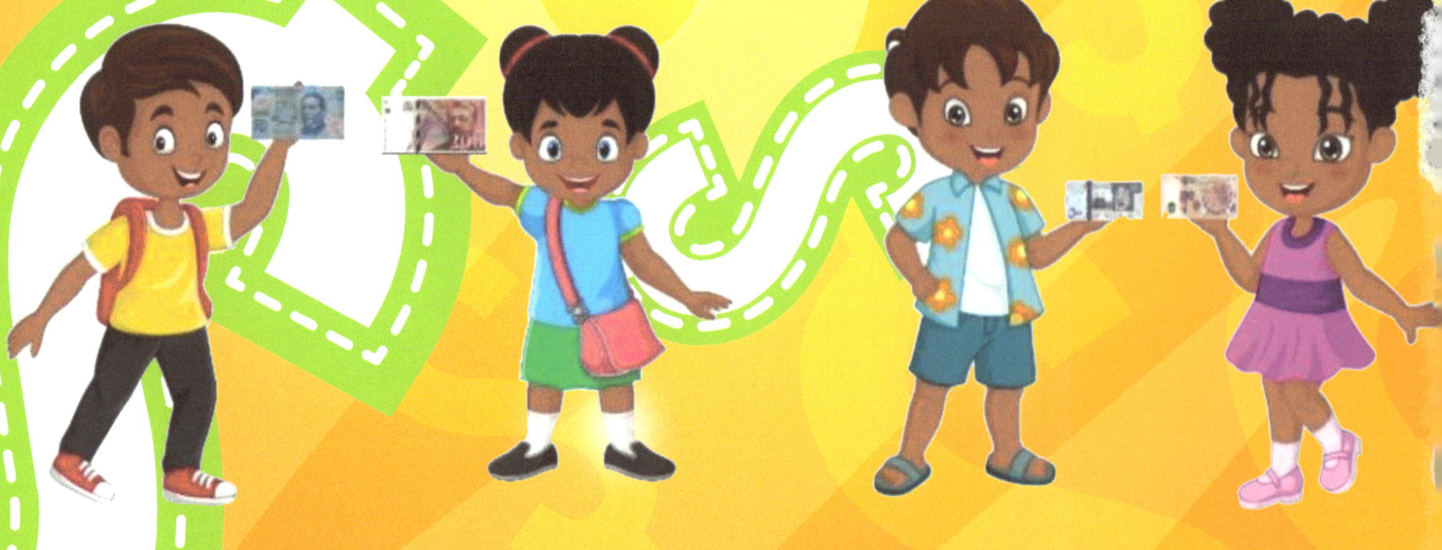

What is money language?

Money language is a special way of talking and sharing ideas about money. It helps us understand and explain things related to money.

Money language is a special way to talk about money. How do you see money? Do you know how you use money can show who you are? It's like using money to express yourself!

To show that you are really good with money and know how to make smart choices. You can wear designer clothes made by famous designers without spending a lot of money. Or, you can make an outfit that looks just like designer clothes but

costs less. Really good but not as expensive.

Money language goes beyond material nature and influences our emotional well-being.

Four Money Languages- Which Language Do You Speak?

Let's explore the different ways people think about money:

1. Driver
2. Amiable
3. Analytic
4. Expressive

The Driver sees money as a path to success. They might feel sad when they don't have much money.

The Amiable find it hard to show love when they don't have much money. They're kind and generous but not always great at planning for the future.

The Analytic thinks of money as a way to stay safe from life's challenges.

The Expressive money language is important to be accepted, and they tend to purchase the respect and admiration of others.

They spend money to fit in with a special group and hide their own worries and insecurities.

Goals

Goals are like a compass that will direct you toward your greatness. Your goal must be to be wealthy. You must decide. When you decide to have money and success, you begin to take immediate action to have riches.

You must choose to BE rich and DO actions to HAVE the money you desire. Desire is the energy that is needed to keep moving toward your goal.

Linda- What are your goals, Scott?

Scott- Well, Linda, goals are exciting things we want to achieve. I aim to save up a lot of money, get a bike, a new phone, and $200!

Linda- Wow, those sound like awesome goals, Scott!

Scott- What about you, Linda? What are your goals?

Linda- What's a goal?

Scott- Goals are like special things you aim for, the things you really want.

Jane- You know, it's a good idea to write down your goals and why you want them. The more reasons you have, the better your chances of achieving your goals. And here's a secret: sometimes, it's best to keep your goals to yourself.

Actions That Will Make You Rich

Linda- A secret? Why, Jane?

Jane- Well, when you know why you want something, you work harder to make it happen. For example, one of my goals is to own a bright red 10-speed bike with white handlebars and a comfy white seat. I want the bike to ride with my friends on sunny days. Another reason is I want to start my very own errand delivery service.

Linda- Wow, those sound amazing!

Jane- And keeping your goals a secret can help you stay focused. Sometimes, if you tell others, they might say things that make you feel sad. It's better to be happy and excited about your goals.

Scott- Having reasons for your goals helps you stay on track. It's like following a map to a hidden treasure. When you know what you want, make decisions, and take the right actions, you're on your way to achieving your goals.

Jane- The four steps of accomplishing my goals are:

1. Decide what I want.
2. Write the goal on my paper.
3. Write the reason.
4. Look at the written goals daily.
5. Keep the goals a secret until I complete the goals.

Linda- Why should I think about my goals every day?

Jane- Think of your goals like a treasure map, Linda. It helps you stay on the right path to find your goals.

Scott- And when you achieve your goals, your confidence grows. The more goals you achieve, the stronger your self-belief becomes!

What goals do you wish to achieve?

____

____

Chapter 4

Believe

In a town where kids had big dreams, four friends had a conversation about something very special one sunny day. They talked about something called "belief.

Belief- A thought that you think constantly and believe to be true.

Terry- I believe I can be rich because I always do my homework.

Ricky- I believe I can be rich because I'm kind and respectful to everyone.

Scott- I believe I can be rich just because I say so!

Linda- Huh? What do you mean, Scott? Why do you believe that?

Scott- Sometimes, you don't need a reason. You need the strong desire and the belief that you deserve to be rich.

Linda- You mean all we have to do is believe we deserve to be rich?

Scott- Yes, it can come true when you truly believe in something you desire.

Together- "Everyone deserves to be rich, no matter their age, height, where they live, or their nationality and race."

Scott- It's like a gift we're born with. We all have the right to be rich.

Terry- Wait, how are we born rich? Are we really born rich?

Scott- Of course! We're all born with the potential to achieve great things.

Scott- So, all we have to do is believe in ourselves and our dreams?

Linda- Exactly. When you desire something and believe in it with all your heart, you can make it happen.

Together- "And remember, you can't be rich only if you decide that you can't be."

Scott- Your positive energy is like magic. It can change your life for the better.

In this town, these friends learned that they could make their dreams come true with belief and determination. So, believe in yourself and your dreams, and who knows what amazing things you can achieve!

Write down your goals for the next day before bed and take action.

Chapter 5

Thoughts & Words

Jane - I can't be rich. I live in a tough neighborhood. My mom and dad work really hard, but we're not rich.

Scott- Nobody becomes rich just by trading their time for money. Having a job means you trade time for money. Becoming rich is about using your money wisely, not working harder.

Jane- How do you use money wisely?

Scott- Well, having two jobs is tough, but you can make your money work for you.

Jane- How can money work?

Scott- Money is like a tool you can use to buy the things you need and want. Money can grow if you use it the right way.

Jane- How can I make money grow?

Scott- By saving money and investing it. Don't spend all your money; put some in a savings account at the bank.

Jane- That sounds like a good idea. Do you have more ideas for making money grow, Scott?

Scott- Yes, you can invest in yourself. There are two ways to do that. The first is by learning and improving yourself, like developing good habits and self-confidence.

Jane- How can I invest in myself?

Scott- By reading books that help you feel good about yourself. When you believe in yourself, you're more likely to succeed in life. Confidence is like a key to unlocking your potential. You can build your confidence by achieving your goals, big or small. If you can do one thing, you can do something else.

The second way is by investing a little money to get more in return. When you buy shares in a company, you help that company grow. In return, they share some of their earnings with you, which is called "dividends."

Jane - **Dividends?**

Scott**- Dividends are the money the company gives you for owning their stock.**

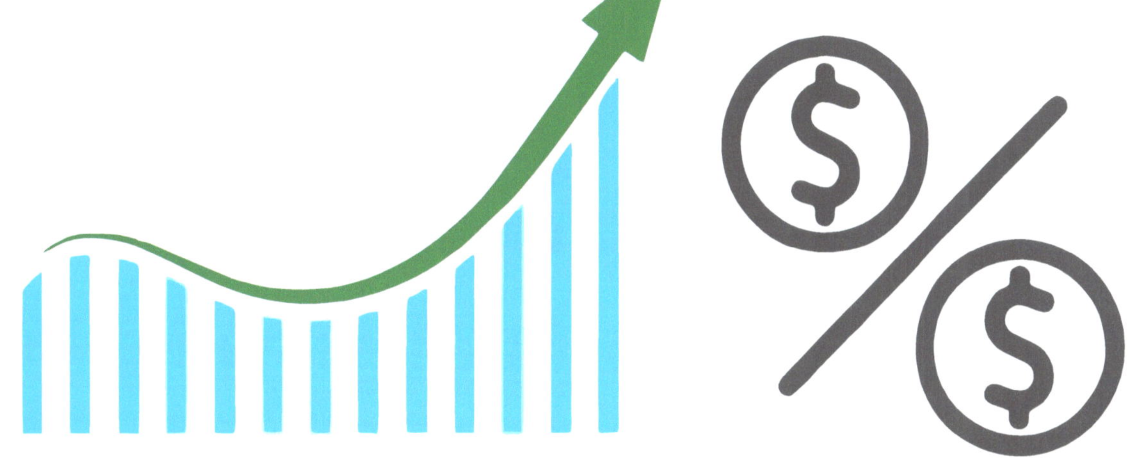

Jane**- When can I start investing? What company should I invest in?**

Scott**- The real magic is in how you think about yourself. The more you fill your mind with positive thoughts about yourself and money, the more you'll grow mentally and financially. Investing takes time, but it's worth the effort and patience.**

Chapter 6

Act As If

Molly- I am a wealthy businesswoman.

William- No, you are not. You are a 10-year-old kid with a briefcase.

Molly- I am a wealthy businesswoman who owns lots of properties, houses, and buildings.

Matthew- She is playing the "Act As If" game.

William- Why?

Matthew- Well, the more you pretend and practice, the closer you get to becoming what you dream of being.

William- How?   **Matthew**- One word.

William-What's the word?   **Matthew**- Imagination

Chapter 7

Plan, Prepare, and Succeed

Jane- Every day, the things you do can help you succeed. Having a daily routine is a great way to start!

Scott- Jane, what's your morning routine like?

Successful people plan and get ready the night before. It's fun to pick out your clothes for the next day and ensure they're clean and neat. Don't forget to finish your homework and put your books in your backpack. You can even make a "Get To Do" list for the next day.

Jane- Planning ahead helps you get ready for success!

Linda- Why is it important to start now, Scott?

- Well, there's no better time than right now. Do you really want to wait until you're much older to achieve your dreams?

For example, if I start saving just $10 a day when I'm 10 years old, by the time I'm 13, I'll have this much. But if I wait until I'm 20, I'll have less.

The decision to start is the first step in reaching your goals. The sooner you figure out what you want in life...

- The closer you are to becoming the person you want to be and doing the things you love. It's all about deciding who you want to be and what you want to do to make your dreams come true.

Chapter 8

What If

Jane- Hey, Linda, let's play the "What If" game.

Linda- I've never heard of the "What If" game.

Jane- It's a fun game where you ask questions about things, places, and people you'd like to experience. You must start every question with "What if?" Then, use your imagination to see yourself having what you truly desire and imagine how you'd feel if you had it. Finally, think about the good things you would do for others once you receive what you want. To finish the game, say, "Thank you" for whatever you imagine.

Linda- Why should I say thank you?

Jane- Well, saying thank you helps your imagination believe that what you want already exists. You wouldn't thank anyone or anything unless they were right there.

Linda- I want $100. What if I had $100?

I want a 10-speed red bike with white trimming and a black leather seat.

Scott- What would you do with your bike? Would you do nice things for others if you had a bike?

Linda- Wow, that sounds like a lot of fun. It feels good to imagine having everything you want and doing all the things you said you would. Then, they can come true.

Linda- It is, but there's one more step to winning the game. It's a top-secret step.

Jane- Top secret?

Linda- Yes.

Jane- Tell me! I promise I won't share your secret.

Linda- It's the magical feeling of desire, like magic; whatever you want will appear. But it takes practice to win. Most people don't win the game because they start to doubt if their wishes will come true.

Jane- Have you ever won the "What If" game, Linda?

Linda- Yes, everything you desire is already yours. It's just waiting for you to believe it and to simply say thank you.

Scott- Hi Linda, my mom wanted me to give you this $100. She saw you cleaning Mrs. Sallory's house after her teenage granddaughter and her friends left a mess. She was so happy to see someone do a good deed, and you cleaned up so nicely without knowing someone was watching.

Jane- You're really good at the "What If" game.

Linda- Practice makes perfect.

Jane- Can I play the "What If" game alone?

Linda- Sure, sometimes it's even better to play alone because you can focus better and enjoy the feeling without any distractions.

Chapter 9

Self Love & Riches

Love is like a warm, cozy blanket that helps your parents wake up each day, working hard for you. They want to ensure you have everything you need, like yummy food, clean water, a safe home, and comfy clothes.

When you do nice things for others, it's like throwing a boomerang of kindness. The good feeling you get from helping someone comes right back to you.

Being kind to others also makes you feel awesome about yourself. It's like having a friendly shadow that follows you everywhere.

Every morning when you wake up, you get to choose to be a great person to yourself and others.

Jane- How can I be kind to myself and others?

Linda- You can start by giving yourself high fives as soon as you wake up.

Jane- High fives? How?

Linda- High fives are like giving yourself happy words. Before you get dressed or wash your face, look at yourself in the mirror and say, 'I am amazing.' Then, share five reasons you're amazing and should be kind to yourself.

Jane- When I wake up, I'll say, 'I am strong, I am happy, I am nice, I am beautiful, and I am love.' I'll also quietly say, 'Be still and know that I am.'

Linda - That's fantastic! But what if I can't think of five good things?

Jane- There's no such thing as 'can't.' If you don't want to feel sad or defeated, stop saying 'I can't' before trying. Start with easy things, like being grateful for having five fingers and a hand.

Jane- You can say, 'I'm happy to have fingers,' 'I can paint pretty nail polish on my nails,' 'I have knuckles to make a fist,' 'I can wave hello to people,' and 'I can brighten someone's day.' Everything you need is right there in your hand.

Linda- Wow, I didn't realize how amazing I am!

Jane- You are amazing! When you look in the mirror and feel confident, you'll notice that others treat you with confidence, too. Connecting with the love inside, you'll attract wonderful things like money,

success, great friendships, and love.

Scott- Remember, when you smile, the whole world smiles with you. So, smile more every day. You're like the sun, spreading happiness, joy, and love to yourself and everyone around you. You don't have to wait for the sun to shine; you are the sunshine!

- Keep thinking good thoughts; you'll see amazing things happen. Your kind thoughts connect to your feelings, and that's when you take action to get what you want. Feeling good attracts positive energy.

Doctor Visits

Scott- Remember, your health is like a hidden treasure. Without the riches of good health, you will be poor. People seldom smile or are happy while physically or mentally sick.

Caring for your mind and body is extremely important to preserve your health and live a long, happy, and prosperous life. To stay healthy, don't forget to see your doctor regularly.

Jane- Meet Dr. Sun! Sun is a booster because it provides vitamin D and fights sadness and nervousness. Dr. Sun brings you energy and joy.

Basking in the sun rays, laying in the grass, and allowing the sun to heal you internally.

Linda- Dr. Nutrition is all about yummy, healthy food. Eating veggies, fruits, and protein helps your body handle stress and stay in good shape. Drinking water is like a magic potion; it cleans your body and keeps you hydrated and feeling great.

- Dr. Exercise wants you to play and move every day! It makes your muscles strong and helps you think better. And guess what? Being active can help you achieve amazing things. So, don't forget to wake up early and get moving!

- Dr. You- Believe it or not, did you know giving to others is more rewarding than giving yourself? When you give authenticity, you are raising the highest vibration- love.

Also, praise yourself and discuss the good things that happen daily. Be grateful for simply being you.

X'ernona- Read "You Can Be Rich Too! "as often as possible and take action towards building wealth daily through positive belief and healthy money habits like paying yourself first, starting a business, and investing.

Remember to change your thoughts, words, and feelings to be focused on prosperity, happiness, joy, success, and money.

Read books that nourish your mind. Take time away from your electrical devices and hang out with positive friends who only want the best for you. Lastly, go for a walk and breathe in the air while reciting the following powerful affirmation:

I am grateful now that abundance comes to me easily and effortlessly on a consistent and everyday basis.

I am receiving. I am receiving it now. I am receiving all the wealth the universe has for me now.